ALL AROUND THE WORLD
CAMBODIA

by Kristine Spanier, MLIS

pogo

Ideas for Parents and Teachers

Pogo Books let children practice reading informational text while introducing them to nonfiction features such as headings, labels, sidebars, maps, and diagrams, as well as a table of contents, glossary, and index.

Carefully leveled text with a strong photo match offers early fluent readers the support they need to succeed.

Before Reading

- "Walk" through the book and point out the various nonfiction features. Ask the student what purpose each feature serves.
- Look at the glossary together. Read and discuss the words.

Read the Book

- Have the child read the book independently.
- Invite him or her to list questions that arise from reading.

After Reading

- Discuss the child's questions. Talk about how he or she might find answers to those questions.
- Prompt the child to think more. Ask: What did you know about Cambodia before reading this book? What more would you like to know after reading it?

Pogo Books are published by Jump!
5357 Penn Avenue South
Minneapolis, MN 55419
www.jumplibrary.com

Library of Congress Cataloging-in-Publication Data

Names: Spanier, Kristine, author.
Title: Cambodia / by Kristine Spanier.
Description: Minneapolis, MN: Jump!, Inc., [2021]
Series: All around the world | Pogo Books
Audience: Ages 7-10 | Audience: Grades 2-3
Identifiers: LCCN 2019035848 (print)
LCCN 2019035849 (ebook)
ISBN 9781645273233 (hardcover)
ISBN 9781645273240 (paperback)
ISBN 9781645273257 (ebook)
Subjects: LCSH: Cambodia—Juvenile literature.
Classification: LCC DS554.3 .S73 2021 (print)
LCC DS554.3 (ebook) | DDC 959.6—dc23
LC record available at https://lccn.loc.gov/2019035848
LC ebook record available at https://lccn.loc.gov/2019035849

Editor: Jenna Gleisner
Designer: Molly Ballanger

Photo Credits: Sergey Peterman/Shutterstock, cover; Sergio de Flore/Shutterstock, 1; Pixfiction/Shutterstock, 3; Dmitry Rukhlenko/Shutterstock, 4; LordRunar/iStock, 5; Nhut Minh Ho/Shutterstock, 6-7; SL-Photography/Shutterstock, 8-9; David Bokuchava/Shutterstock, 10; E Ford/Shutterstock, 11; vovashevchuk/iStock, 12-13tl; ePhotocorp/iStock, 12-13tr; Narupon Nimpaiboon/Shutterstock, 12-13bl; Guek Hock Ping/Photoshot NHPA/SuperStock, 12-13br; Tran Qui Thinh/Shutterstock, 14-15; Mirrorpix/Getty, 16; Jeff_Cagle/iStock, 17; OULAILAX NAKHONE/Shutterstock, 18-19; Agencja Fotograficzna Caro/Alamy, 20-21; Henning Marquardt/Shutterstock, 23.

Printed in the United States of America at Corporate Graphics in North Mankato, Minnesota.

TABLE OF CONTENTS

CHAPTER 1

WELCOME TO CAMBODIA!

Travel down the Mekong River. Visit the Royal Palace. Count the faces on the Bayon **Temple**. There are 216 of them! Welcome to Cambodia!

Bayon Temple

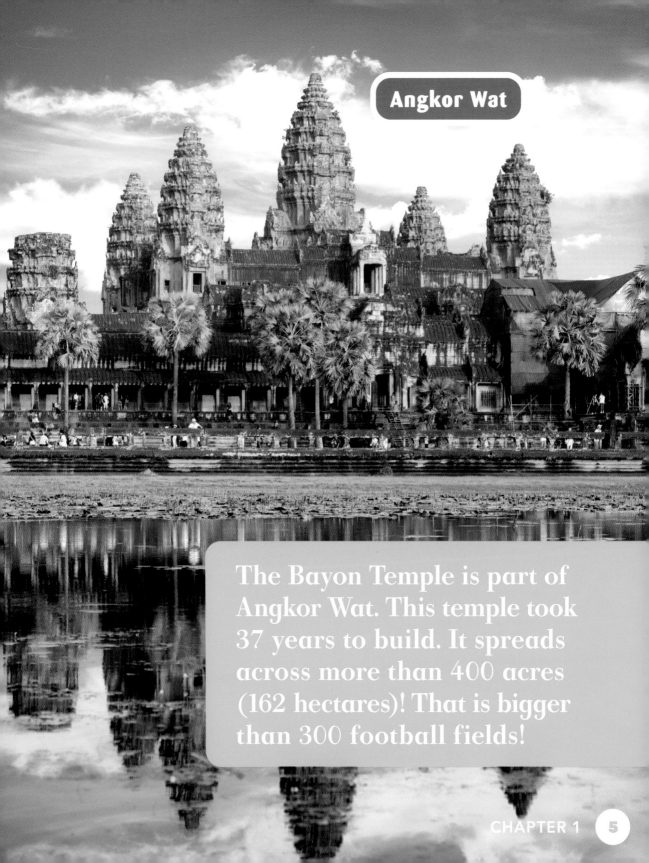

Angkor Wat

The Bayon Temple is part of Angkor Wat. This temple took 37 years to build. It spreads across more than 400 acres (162 hectares)! That is bigger than 300 football fields!

Phnom Penh

A king rules this country. He chooses a **prime minister**. This person is the head of the government.

The National Assembly has 125 members. The Senate has 61 members. They meet in Phnom Penh. This is the **capital**.

WHAT DO YOU THINK?

Angkor Wat is on the country flag. It is the only country flag that has a building on it. What does your country's flag have on it? If you could design one, what would you put on it? Why?

The Royal Palace is also in Phnom Penh. It was built in 1866. Kings have lived and worked here. The Throne Hall was built in 1917. It is used for religious and royal **ceremonies**. Guests of the king meet here, too.

Throne Hall

CHAPTER 2

CLIMATE AND WILDLIFE

It is never cold in Cambodia! Temperatures are around 80 to 95 degrees Fahrenheit (27 to 35 degrees Celsius). The rainy season is from May to November.

Water rises in Tonle Sap Lake. Homes nearby are on **stilts**. The lake is full of fish.

stilt

king cobra

banded krait

large-eyed green pit viper

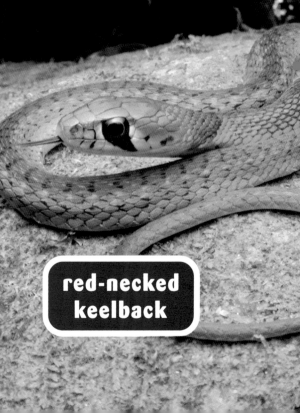

red-necked keelback

Tigers and leopards prowl the country. Herons and cranes fly in the sky. Four different kinds of dangerous snakes live here, too.

Cambodia has seven national parks! Plants and animals are protected in them. The Preah Monivong Bokor National Park is in the Cardamom Mountains.

A statue is in this park. It is of Lok Yeay Mao. The statue stands for protection. It is 95 feet (29 meters) tall!

DID YOU KNOW?

The tallest peak in this park is Phnom Bokor. It is 3,547 feet (1,081 m) high!

Lok Yeay Mao

CHAPTER 3

LIFE IN CAMBODIA

The Khmer Rouge ruled the country from 1975 to 1979. This group was violent. It wanted Cambodia to become **communist**. The group **forbade** religions. It destroyed schools and hospitals.

rice farming

People were forced to leave cities. They moved to **rural** areas. They farmed for a living.

In 1991, a **peace agreement** was signed. A new government was put into place.

Many people here still farm rice. It is an **export**.

TAKE A LOOK!

A **majority** of the **population** still lives in rural areas. The rest live in **urban** areas.

76.6%
rural population

23.4%
urban population

Many students only attend school until fifth grade. It can be hard to get to school. Some kids are needed at home to help with chores.

People here like many sports. Some like to kickbox. They might play badminton or tennis. Others like to watch motocross races.

What would you like to do or see in Cambodia?

WHAT DO YOU THINK?

Can you imagine only going to school through fifth grade? Would you like this? Why or why not?

QUICK FACTS & TOOLS

CAMBODIA

Location: Southeast Asia

Size: 69,898 square miles
(181,035 square kilometers)

Population: 16,449,519
(July 2018 estimate)

Capital: Phnom Penh

Type of Government:
parliamentary constitutional
monarchy

Language: Khmer

Exports: clothing, footwear,
timber, rubber, rice, fish, tobacco

Currency: Cambodian riel

GLOSSARY

capital: A city where government leaders meet.

ceremonies: Formal events that mark important occasions.

communist: A type of government in which all land, property, businesses, and resources belong to the government.

export: A product sold to different countries.

forbade: Ordered not to do something.

majority: More than half of the people in a group.

peace agreement: An agreement between two or more hostile parties, usually countries or governments, which formally ends a state of war.

population: The total number of people who live in a place.

prime minister: The leader of a country.

rural: Related to the country and country life.

stilts: Posts that hold a structure above the ground or water level.

temple: A building used for worship.

urban: Related to the city and city life.

Cambodia's currency

INDEX

TO LEARN MORE

Finding more information is as easy as 1, 2, 3.

1 Go to www.factsurfer.com

2 Enter "Cambodia" into the search box.

3 Click the "Surf" button to see a list of websites.

FACT SURFER